History in Evidence

MEDIEVAL BRITAIN

Robin Place

Wayland

History in Evidence

Cover design: Alison Anholt-White
Series design: Helen White
Consultant: Dr Margaret L Faull

Cover pictures: The main picture is Conwy Castle in Gwynedd. The inset is a pilgrim's badge.

First published in 1989 by
Wayland (Publishers) Limited
61 Western Road, Hove
East Sussex BN3 1JD, England

British Library Cataloguing in Publication Data
Place, Robin
   Medieval Britain. – (History in evidence)
   1. Great Britain, 1154–1485
   I. Title II. Series
   941.03

   ISBN 1-85210-578-X

Edited and typeset by Kudos, Hove, East Sussex
Printed in Italy by G. Canale & C.S.p.A., Turin
Bound in France by A.G.M.

Picture acknowlegements
The publishers would like to thank the following for permission to reproduce their illustrations on the pages mentioned: Ashmolean Museum, Oxford 8; Cambridge University Collection: copyright reserved 10; City of Birmingham Museum 11 (lower); Malcolm Cooper/Birmingham University Field Archaeology Unit 6; Elizabeth Eames 19 (upper); James Greig 9; Museum of London 20 (inset), 22 (both), 26 (both), 27 (upper); Norfolk Museums Service 11 (upper: Norwich Castle Museum), 17 (lower: King's Lynn Museums); Northamptonshire County Council Archaeology Unit 19 (lower: Christopher Addison-Jones); Robin Place 29 (both); Ronald Sheridan/The Ancient Art & Architecture Collection 17 (upper), 23; Skyscan *cover* (main picture); TOPHAM *cover* (inset), 7 (both), 24, 28; Weald & Downland Open Air Museum 13; Winchester Excavations Committee 14; Winchester Museums Service 15 (upper: R Kipling; lower: M Barden). The artwork was supplied by: Malcolm S Walker 4, 18, 27; Stephen Wheele 10, 13, 16 (after Stuart Rigold), 20, 21, 25.

Contents

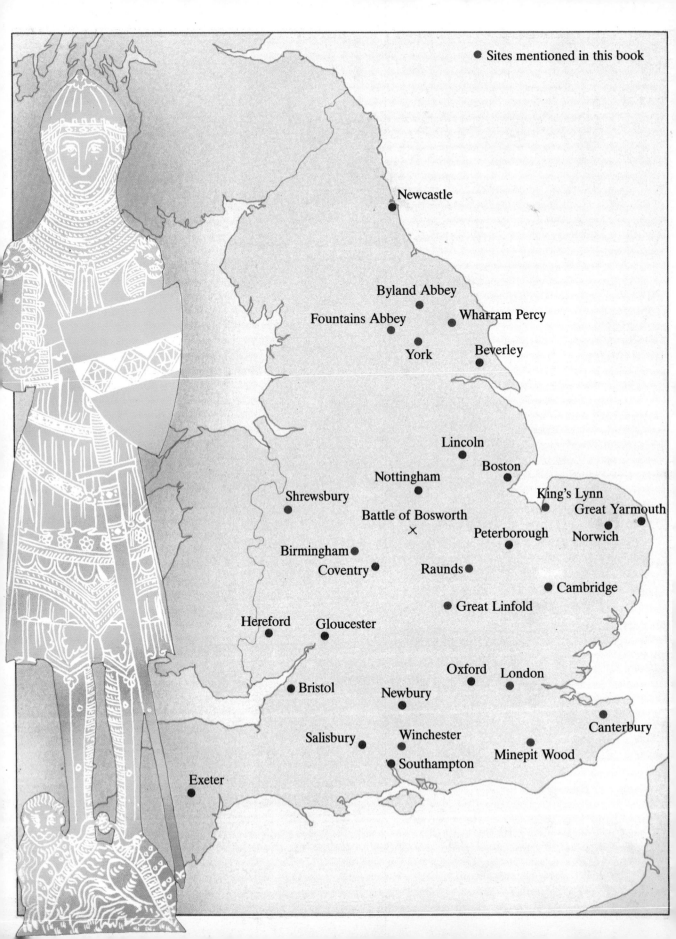

Sites mentioned in this book

Newcastle

Byland Abbey

Fountains Abbey

Wharram Percy

York

Beverley

Lincoln

Boston

Nottingham

King's Lynn

Shrewsbury

Great Yarmouth

Battle of Bosworth

Peterborough

Norwich

Birmingham

Coventry

Raunds

Cambridge

Great Linfold

Hereford

Gloucester

Oxford

London

Bristol

Newbury

Canterbury

Salisbury

Winchester

Minepit Wood

Southampton

Exeter

Introducing the Middle Ages

The years from 1300 to 1485 are known as the Middle Ages. During this time, most people were peasants who worked on the land. Their life was hard and painful. Often, harvests were ruined by bad weather and they died of starvation. Terrible plagues, too, carried by the fleas of the black rat, killed thousands of people.

Food, produced by the peasants, fed craftsmen living in towns. These towns became important centres through which the country was governed.

Everyone went to church often. The sick believed that they could be cured by praying at the shrines of saints. Chaucers's *The Canterbury Tales* describes pilgrims going to the shrine of St Thomas Becket in Canterbury, Kent. Some pilgrims even went as far as Jerusalem.

Many churches, monasteries and nunneries were built, using money and land given to the Church. Bishops were important landowners, so were some priests. Clever boys became monks and learned to read and write. Some could have a good career in charge of the Church's land, even becoming advisers to the king.

Boys of noble families learned to fight according to the rules of chivalry, and became knights. They kept in training by jousting at tournaments.

Many castles were built to control the land around them. They were important during the wars between the British and the Welsh and the Scots, and in the Wars of the Roses, when rivals fought to be King of England.

OPPOSITE This map shows the main towns and cities in Britain during the Middle Ages. All the places mentioned in this book are marked in red.

The Middle Ages 1300–1485

1272–1307	Reign of Edward I who fought the Scots and the Welsh.
1337	Start of the Hundred Years War with France.
1348–49	The Black Death – a plague that killed nearly half the population.
1381	The Peasants' Revolt, led by Wat Tyler.
1455	The start of the Wars of the Roses. The Duke of York fought the Lancastrian King Henry VI.
1461	The end of the Wars of the Roses. Edward IV became king.
1484	Murder of the little princes in the Tower of London.
1485	Richard III killed at the Battle of Bosworth. Henry VII becomes the first Tudor king. End of the Middle Ages.

Finding the Middle Ages

Excavating a monastery in Shrewsbury. Houses and railway tracks had been built over it, but as the area was being redeveloped, archaeologists had a chance to dig. Here they have uncovered the stone walls of a kitchen.

There are three ways of finding out about the Middle Ages. Firstly, we can visit churches, castles and other buildings that are still standing.

Secondly, there are documents that tell us the names of people and what they did. Drawings show what people looked like and the things they used.

Thirdly, archaeologists dig up things people made, and find out how craftsmen worked. They dig up the remains of buildings too. In towns, documents may give the name and work of the owners of plots of land, so archaeologists can tell whose house they are digging up and can show how it altered over the years.

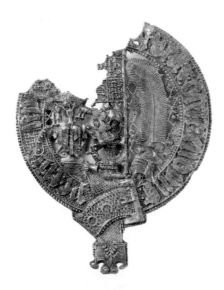

ABOVE People wore badges, like this one, to show that they had visited a holy place.

Wet finds
Water in an excavation makes digging unpleasant and difficult but wet ground means that wood, leather and food are preserved, and can be studied in the laboratory after the dig.

This is Scotney Castle, near Lamberhurst in Kent. Many of its rooms have survived, so we have a good idea of what it was like to live there during the Middle Ages.

Food and drink

Manuscripts tell us about the food eaten by the rich, and how it was cooked and served. In one castle drain, archaeologists found the remains of 20 different kinds of fish, 9 kinds of meat – including venison (from deer), rabbit and hare – and birds, such as goose, dove, grouse, partridge, moorhen, thrush, redwing and blue tit. Some of this food was provided by hunting and hawking.

Excavation is especially important for the information it gives about the food of ordinary people. At King's Lynn, in Norfolk, animal bones from rubbish pits showed that people ate much more beef than mutton or pork. They also ate a lot of goose at meal-times.

People ate plenty of fish, especially on Fridays and during Lent. Cod, herring, haddock, plaice, whiting and mackerel were caught in nets at sea. Eels and salmon were caught in rivers, but even in the Middle Ages some rivers were to polluted for certain fish that had been caught

Environmental archaeology
Seeds, bits of plants and fish bones are sieved by archaeologists from the wet mud of cesspits and drains and examined under microscopes in laboratories. This work is called 'environmental archaeology', and gives us useful evidence of what people ate in the Middle Ages.

A puzzle jug. It was made in about 1300, and found in Oxford. It has two spouts. If a person lifted the wrong spout to their lips, the other spout poured wine all over their clothes, which made everyone laugh!

in earlier times. Great houses and monasteries had their own fish-ponds, which people had dug. At Byland Abbey, in Yorkshire, the monks built a dam across a valley to make a fish-pond, and then sold fish to earn money.

Meat and fish were preserved by smoking and salting, and served with herbs and spices. Monks, nuns and poor people ate a lot of pottage, which was a thick soup made with grain and vegetables. Few vegetables leave traces in the ground, but archaeologists have found the remains of leeks and broad beans.

Illness
Parasite eggs have been found in the remains of food, which tell us that many people had worms living in their insides. These would have made them feel uncomfortable and cross!

Towards the end of the Middle Ages, people complained that monks and nuns were becoming less holy. Archaeologists have discovered from food remains that some were certainly changing to more expensive food and eating meat.

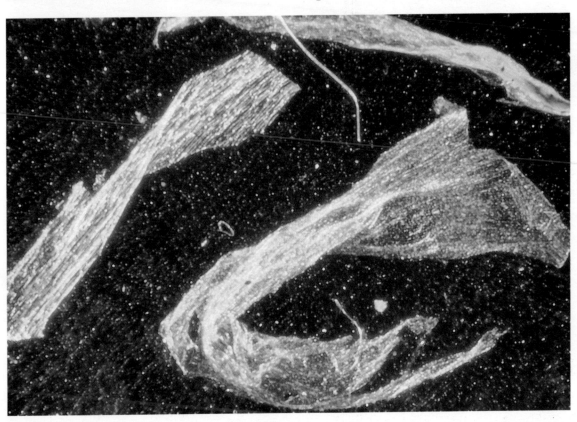

Pieces of an onion leaf seen through a microscope. They were found in the excavations of a rubbish pit in Chester. Scientists have dated them to the Middle Ages.

A castle kitchen

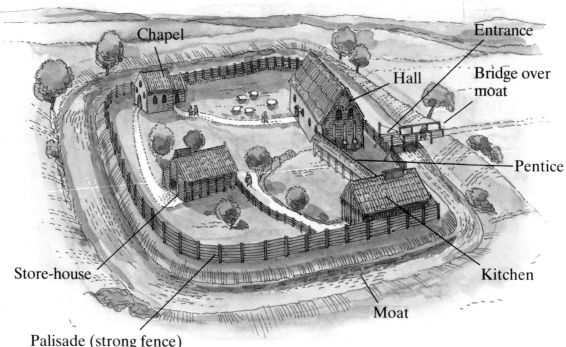

Chapel

Entrance

Hall

Bridge over moat

Pentice

Store-house

Kitchen

Moat

Palisade (strong fence)

Weoley Castle in the Middle Ages. A wooden passageway, called a 'pentice', leads from the wooden kitchen to the stone-built hall where the food was eaten.

Castle walls and keeps (well-protected towers) were built of stone, and many are still standing. But the courtyards in castles that are now grassy spaces were once filled with wooden buildings that have rotted away. Archaeologists excavate these courtyards to find the remains of stables, kitchens and store-rooms, as they tell us a lot about life in castles.

In 1960, a wooden kitchen was excavated at Weoley Castle, Birmingham, about 2.5 m below the present ground level. It was an especially exciting dig, because 1-m high walls of planks, slotted into upright posts, were found still standing. The wood was preserved because the ground was wet and also because, when people stopped using the kitchen, wet clay from the moat was dumped over it, preventing it from decaying.

The kitchen was 12.5 m long and 6.8 m wide. In one corner was a big hearth, built of two layers of sandstone blocks, where meat could be roasted and food boiled in cauldrons. Near the hearth was a stony floor for the washing-up.

A bronze skillet (a pan used for cooking) excavated at King's Lynn, in Norfolk.

Archaeologists found bits of the roof on the floor. It was made of reeds laid on top of branches that had been woven together. Broken cooking pots, lost coins and old shoes, left behind by the men who did the cooking, were also discovered by the archaeologists.

RIGHT Part of the wooden wall of the kitchen at Weoley Castle, which was uncovered by archaeologists in 1960.

The countryside

The deserted village of Wharram Percy, Yorkshire, seen from the air, with its houses and roads shown by earthworks.

Many villages were abandoned because of bad harvests and plagues. If the site has not been ploughed up or built over, the outline of the village can still be seen, especially from the air.

Archaeologists have found that the layout of a village was always changing. Houses needed rebuilding, and the owners would choose a new site. In the west and north of Britain, houses were built of stone. If there was no building-stone, houses were made of oak timbers, with walls of wattle and daub, and a thatched roof. If the wall-posts were set in holes in the ground, the posts would rot in about twenty years. But if the posts stood on flat slabs, called pad-stones, the house would last for about fifty years.

Bricks, brought from northern Europe, were used for some grand buildings in eastern England from the thirteenth century onwards. However, small houses were not built of bricks until after the end of the Middle Ages.

ABOVE A farmhouse re-erected at the Weald and Downland Museum in West Sussex. It shows the timber-framed walls before they were covered with wattle and daub. This house has a smoke-hole, not a chimney.

A clean sweep

Housewives in the Middle Ages kept their floors well-swept. Archaeologists do not find lost objects and bones from meals scattered everywhere, unlike Viking houses in York. Dirty floors give archaeologists more information about how people lived, but in the later Middle Ages the rubbish was tidily put outside. Brooms, made out of twigs, swept away the surface of the clay or beaten-earth floor, as well as the rubbish. The floor gradually sank lower than the ground outside the house. So even if all traces of the wooden walls have vanished, archaeologists can find out how big a house was by measuring the sunken floor.

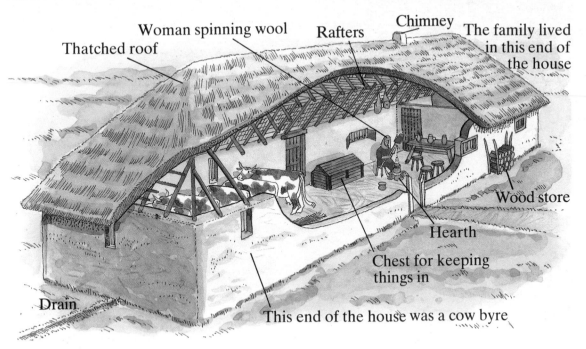

A fifteenth-century peasant's long-house. Having the animals at one end of the house helped to keep it warm. The fire was in the middle of the floor at the other end.

Towns

About 700 towns were built in England during the Middle Ages. Often the land had to be drained, because it was very wet. Then the streets were laid out and surfaced with gravel or cobbles. People rented rectangular plots of land, with one narrow side facing the street, and put a fence round them. (Some of the medieval boundaries around property are still the same today.) On each plot, there was a house or a shop, with a yard behind for outbuildings, a well and rubbish pits.

Many craftsmen worked in towns. This chalk-lined channel, found in Winchester, brought clean water to a fuller's workshop, where woollen cloth was soaked and shrunk to thicken it.

RIGHT This is all that remains of the walls of a house in The Brooks, Winchester, which was excavated by archaeologists. Documents have been found to show that it belonged to someone called John de Tytynge. He was a wool merchant who grew very rich when the weaving industry became important. He became the Mayor of Winchester and he was also elected as a Member of Parliament. He died in 1312.

A reconstruction of John de Tytynge's house. He enlarged it by building a stone hall with a big doorway to link the two shops on the left with the hall on the right. He put in a lavatory upstairs in the end-building on the left. He converted a building at the back into a kitchen.

Especially from the 1400s onwards, documents give information about towns, including street names and the names and occupations of people buying and selling properties. Old maps of some towns show that they changed very little until the 1760s, when there was a lot of building work carried out in the towns.

Excavation in towns began after the Second World War, in the open spaces created by bombing. This type of excavation is very important because archaeologists can discover what town houses were like, and how they have been altered over the years. Also, they can find the houses of the poor, which were not important enough to be described in documents.

Crafts and industries

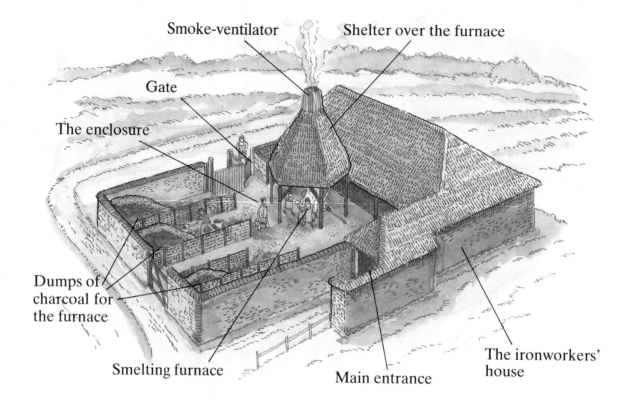

Smoke-ventilator Shelter over the furnace

Gate

The enclosure

Dumps of charcoal for the furnace

Smelting furnace

Main entrance

The ironworkers' house

An iron-working site at Minepit Wood, East Sussex, in the 1300s. Iron ore was roasted in a furnace outside the enclosure. Then it was crushed with hammers into small lumps for smelting in the furnace in the middle of the enclosure.

Mining was important in the Middle Ages. Tin from Devon and Cornwall was sold abroad; lead, from the north of England, was used for roofs, water-pipes and small ornaments, like pilgrim badges.

Stone was dug up for building castles, cathedrals, town walls and a small number of houses. It was transported long distances by wagon and by boat.

The production of iron ore was especially important as it was made into tools for many craftsmen. Charcoal was needed for this, and travelling charcoal burners stacked lengths of wood into a mound and covered it with leaves and earth. They kept a small fire smouldering in the mound for several days. In this way, the wood was turned to charcoal.

A picture from the Middle Ages showing a leatherworker in his workshop.

holders, as well as hinges and padlocks for their doors and wooden chests.

Bronzesmiths made valuable bronze containers, buckles, brooches and church bells. Goldsmiths made jewellery, often with precious stones. Leatherworkers made belts, purses and harnesses, as well as jugs and bottles. Glassmakers could not make pretty glass jugs like the ones imported from Venice, in Italy, but they produced small bottles and glass for church windows. (Glass was only made for house windows towards the end of the 1400s.)

A knife excavated in King's Lynn, Norfolk. The wooden handle was turned on a lathe.

Blacksmiths used iron to make horse-shoes, parts of wagons, rivets for ships, masons' trowels, knives for leatherwork-ers, and axes, adzes, saws, punches, hammers and chisels for woodworkers. Coopers used iron to make buckets and barrels. Carpenters shaped timbers for houses and furniture with their tools. Shipwrights and foresters needed iron tools for their work in building ships and cutting down trees. Householders needed iron cauldrons, cleavers (a heavy knife for chopping up meat), pans and candle-

Pottery and tiles

Clay for making pots is found in many parts of England. Most kilns in the Middle Ages were in the countryside.

Pots were shaped on the potter's wheel. Kitchen pots included cauldrons, pans and dishes. Clay lamps and watering-pots for gardens were made, too, as well as 'curfews' to cover fires safely overnight. Food and liquids were carried to market in big storage jars.

Pots were easily broken. At kiln sites, archaeologists find many broken pieces, or sherds, from 'wasters' – pots that were not good enough to sell. These show what pots were made at that kiln. When archaeologists find the same sherds at other sites, they can work out how far the pots from one kiln have travelled to be sold.

In the southern half of England, as well as roof-tiles, tiles were made for the floors of palaces, churches, castles and, later, grand houses. Some were plain, coloured brown, black, yellow or green. Others had

BELOW   A potter in the Middle Ages would have used a kiln like this one to bake his pots.

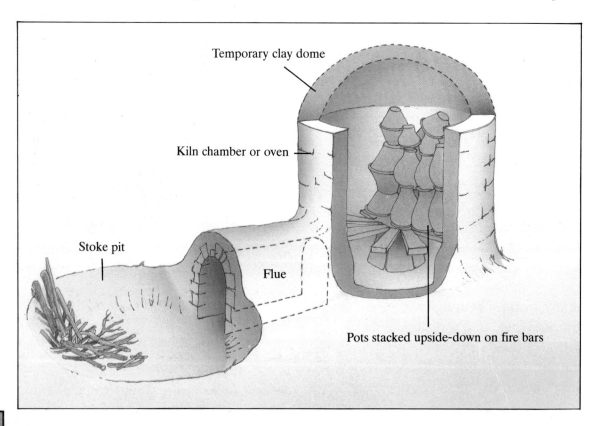

Temporary clay dome

Kiln chamber or oven

Stoke pit

Flue

Pots stacked upside-down on fire bars

patterns with a design in white. This design was pressed into the damp tile with a wooden stamp. Then the tile was glazed and fired in a kiln. Some designs were made up of groups of four, nine or sixteen floor tiles.

Tiled floors were easy to clean. Erasmus, a famous Dutchman, complained of the smell in some English houses from the cat and dog messes and bits of food rotting in the rushes covering the earth floors.

RIGHT A pattern made up of four tiles. This is part of a thirteenth-century floor which was excavated at Rievaulx Abbey, Yorkshire.

Pots from a manor house at Raunds, Northamptonshire. In the centre are shiny green-glazed jugs. The plain vessels are cooking pots and shallow bowls. The green pot in the shape of a ram is an aquamanile. The head is a spout. Aquamaniles were used to pour water over the hands before eating a meal.

Ships and waterfronts

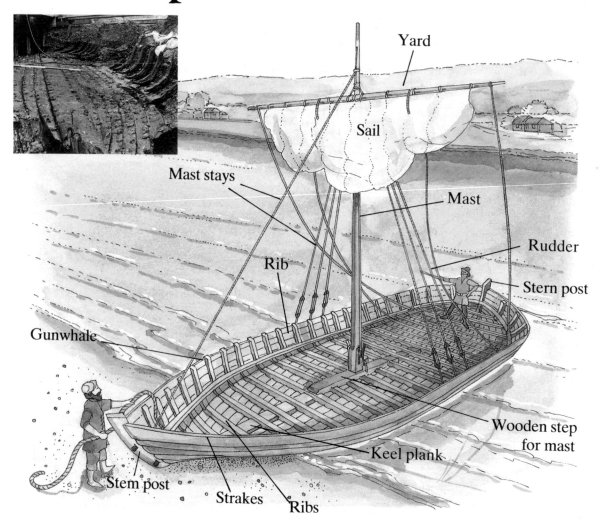

Yard

Sail

Mast stays

Mast

Rudder

Rib

Stern post

Gunwhale

Wooden step for mast

Keel plank

Stem post

Strakes

Ribs

We get some idea of what ships in the Middle Ages looked like from drawings scratched on church pillars and walls. Documents help, too, with drawings of ships' rigging. Inventories also provide us with a list of a ship's equipment. But it is from shipwrecks, preserved in rivers and the sea, that we find out how big ships

This fifteenth-century sailing ship carried goods up and down the River Thames, until it sank at Blackfriars. The ship was excavated by archaeologists in 1970 (top left). It was 16 m long and 3 m wide. Both ends were pointed. The rudder was the large steering oar. The planks of the bottom and sides were riveted together. The strengthening ribs were fastened to the planks by wooden pegs.

were and how they were built. The ropes and sails have been swept away, but the possessions of the crew show what sailors used. These include wood and leather things that have decayed on dry, land sites, but have been preserved in water.

It saved time unloading goods if ships could tie up at a waterfront instead of their cargoes being brought ashore by barges. Many towns built big timber waterfronts out into rivers, filling in the space behind with loads of rubbish. This provided extra land for building warehouses.

The big timbers of the waterfronts are preserved in the wet ground, so archaeologists have been able to study the methods of the carpenters who built them. They have found all sorts of interesting things in the rubbish too, including pottery and leather shoes.

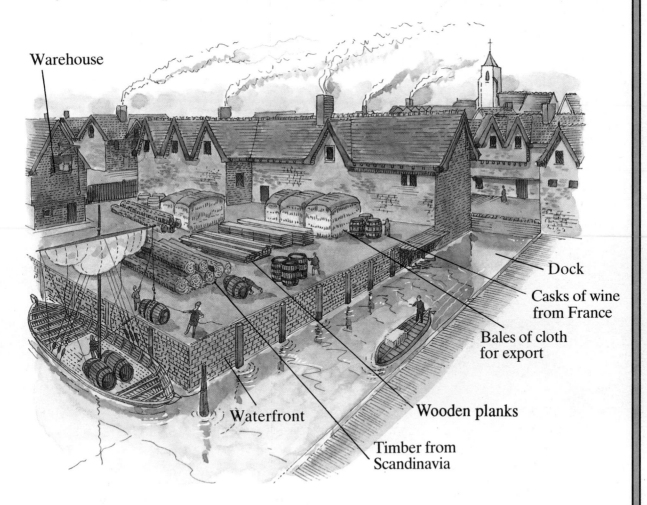

Warehouse

Dock

Casks of wine from France

Bales of cloth for export

Wooden planks

Timber from Scandinavia

Waterfront

As a result of their excavations, archaeologists think that a dock near Blackfriars Bridge in London looked like this in the 1400s.

The wool trade

In the Middle Ages, weavers in Belgium, France, Germany and Italy bought a lot of English wool because it was so good. During the 1300s, the price of wool rose so high that these European weavers stopped buying it. People then began weaving woollen cloth in workshops in England, and woollen cloth became an important export.

Archaeologists are finding out about the different breeds of sheep that produced all this wool. Animal bones from rubbish pits show that sheep were smaller than they are today, and many had horns.

Woollen cloth woven in a way called 'twill' to give diagonal lines, also found in London.

Woollen cloth woven in chequers and dyed red and brown with madder, found in London.

The size of sheepskins made into parchments also shows the small size of sheep in the Middle Ages. Some parchments preserve hair from fleeces, and these are studied under microscopes to show the types of wool which were available then. Several pieces of wool and woven cloth have also been discovered in some wet ground in London.

Archaeologists want to find out more about the making of wool into cloth in the Middle Ages. After shearing, wool was carded and combed. Iron teeth from wooden comb-frames have been found. Wool was spun into yarn using a spindle weighted with a whorl of stone, bone or clay. So many of these have been found that it is unlikely that spinning wheels were used. The wooden looms used for weaving have not survived, but bone weaving tools have been discovered.

A weaver at work on his loom, from a book that was printed in the Middle Ages.

After weaving, the cloth was pounded in water with fuller's earth to thicken it and remove the grease. (A few workshops where this was done have been excavated.) Then the cloth was stretched on frames to dry. The hooks, called tenterhooks, to which it was attached have been found. Dyers' workshops, where the wool or cloth was coloured with dyes, have been excavated.

The monks' woolhouse

In the Middle Ages, many people lived in monasteries and nunneries. They spent a lot of time in prayer, but they also grew their own food and made their own clothes. Travellers stayed in their guest-houses, and the sick were cared for in hospices. Monasteries were the centres of learning, and monks taught boys to read and write.

Many monasteries became very rich from gifts of land and money, and from selling their crops.

Much is known about some parts of monasteries, like the church and dormitories, but we need to find out more about the buildings where the monks worked. At Fountains Abbey, in Yorkshire, a

The remains of Fountains Abbey. In the Middle Ages, its monks kept huge flocks of sheep and cleaned and dyed their wool in a woolhouse.

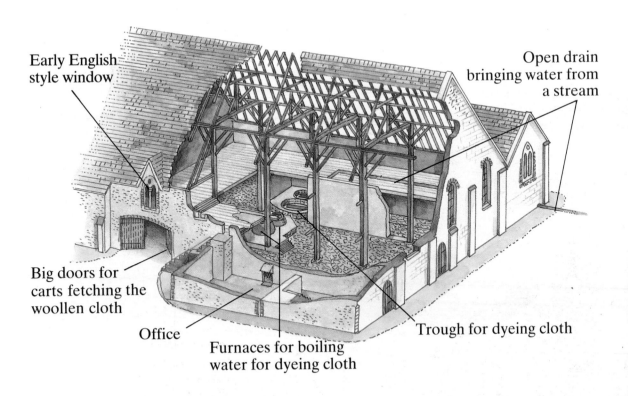

Early English style window

Open drain bringing water from a stream

Big doors for carts fetching the woollen cloth

Office

Furnaces for boiling water for dyeing cloth

Trough for dyeing cloth

A reconstruction of the monks' woolhouse at Fountains Abbey, in Yorkshire.

ruined stone building, which was thought to be a bake-house, was excavated in 1977. The dig showed that the building had had a different use. It had once been a woolhouse where cloth had been processed. Documents about the abbey mentioned 'monks of the woolhouse'. This is where they had worked.

Archaeologists found that an old stone storehouse, built about 1150, had been enlarged in the thirteenth century to make a fulling mill to clean the wool. A water channel, 80 cm wide, brought water from a stream into the woolhouse to work a water-wheel. This powered hammers to pound the cloth in two big, round vats, which were lined with stone.

Early in the fourteenth century, rectangular tanks were put in the vats, and two furnaces (which everyone had previously thought to be ovens for baking bread) were built nearby. The dig showed that these were for boiling water, which was taken in lead pipes to the tanks where the cloth was dyed.

We know from documents that many monasteries kept huge flocks of sheep. The discoveries at Fountains Abbey proved that the monks cleaned and dyed their own wool.

Clothing

ABOVE A man's shoe, called a 'poulaine'. The long point was stuffed with moss (top left) to keep it stiff. The shoe was made of soft goatskin with a leather sole.

Tombs in churches and drawings in manuscripts show what people wore in the Middle Ages, but archaeologists have found a lot of information about clothing from bits of fabric and leather found in wet ground. At Baynard's Castle, in London, 800 shoes were found, along with pieces of cloth, including imported silk, satin, damask and velvet. Most of the pieces were English woollen cloth.

Archaeologists looking at cloth under microscopes have discovered that wool was woven on horizontal looms in workshops, and not at upright looms in people's homes, as in earlier times. They have also discovered that the dyes to colour cloth were made from plants like woad, madder, weld and various lichens. Expensive

The collar of a woollen garment which was cut off when the garment was altered.

RIGHT A woman's hairnet from the 1300s. It was found in London by archaeologists during excavations. It was made from silk thread imported from abroad.

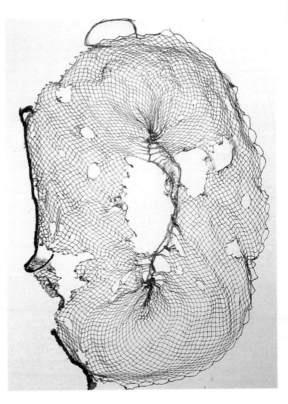

The oldest spectacles in Europe, from about 1440. They were found in rubbish behind a waterfront in Trig Lane, London. They were made of bone from a bull's foot bone. The glass lenses were not found.

imported dyes from Spain, India and Mediterranean countries were used too.

Cloth was cut with iron shears or scissors. Bronze needles and thimbles were used for sewing. Clothes were fastened with bone buttons or laces with bronze tags, and were often lined or decorated with fur. At King's Lynn, in Norfolk, bones of many young cats were found which had been killed for their skins.

Many bronze buckles have been discovered – from belts, armour, spurs and shoes. Archaeologists have also found manicure sets, tweezers, keys and little bells, which once dangled from leather belts. Rich people wore brooches, rings and other jewellery.

The little princes

In 1674, the bones of two children were dug up in the Tower of London. Were they the little princes murdered in 1483? Documents say that the boys were 12 and 10 years old when they died. The age of a child's skeleton can be worked out from the number of second teeth that have replaced milk teeth. We also know that bones join together at different ages in different parts of the body.

It is difficult to say if children's bones are those of a boy or a girl, but bone experts decided recently that the bones from the Tower were of boys who died at about 12 and 10. But were they members of the royal family?

Fortunately, the experts were able to

Victims of the Black Death. A grave, containing the bodies of 762 men, women and children, was found in 1987 near the Tower of London.

Diseases
Archaeologists have examined the skeletons of many medieval people. They can tell from the bones how old people were when they died and, sometimes, what diseases they had suffered from. Only about one in every ten adults lived to be 50. Many babies, children and teenagers died.

We know that people suffered from tuberculosis (a disease of the lungs), leprosy (a skin disease) and osteoarthritis (a disease of the joints between bones). Bad harvests caused malnutrition, rickets and scurvy.

Some skeletons have broken bones that have healed well, showing that splints were used. Many people died violently from sword-cuts, but some healed wounds show that people were looked after carefully.

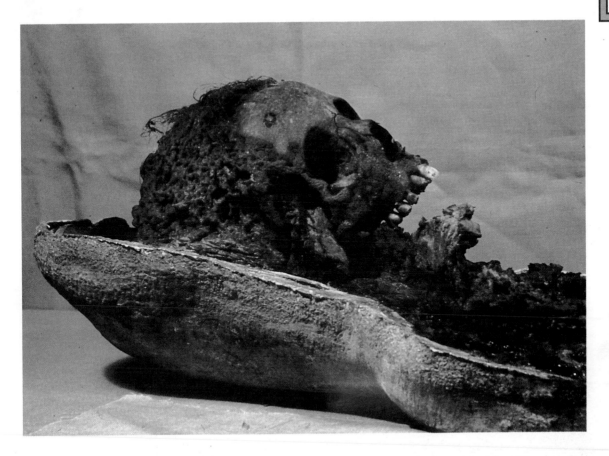

ABOVE   Anne Mowbray's body. BELOW   Comparing her skull and teeth with remains found in the Tower of London helped to confirm that the bones belonged to the princes.

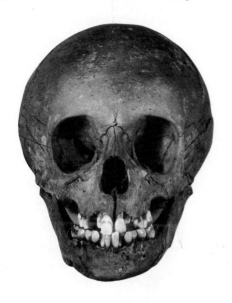

compare the boys' bones with those of Anne Mowbray, a cousin of the two princes, who died when she was 8 years old. Her body was found in a lead coffin in 1965. The experts looked for unusual features in her skeleton that were also in the boys' bones, as these would prove that they were related.

They found family likenesses in the skulls, the teeth and thumb-bones, so it now seems likely that these boys really were the 'little princes'. (But we still do not know who murdered them.)

Places to visit

See what medieval buildings you can find near your home. Look for a castle, an abbey, monastery or nunnery, a cathedral, minster or parish church. There may be medieval houses too. In the countryside, you might find earthworks that are the remains of a deserted village.

Canterbury and York are among towns that have many medieval buildings still standing.

There are many castles to explore, such as Bodiam, in Kent; Carisbrooke, on the Isle of Wight; Dover, in Kent; the Tower of London; and, in North Wales, Caernarvon, Conwy, Harlech and Beaumaris.

Museums

To find things made by medieval craftsmen, try to visit the Museum of London and the British Museum, London. See what medieval things are displayed in your local museum. Excavations have taken place in the following cities, so their museums should have a lot of medieval objects on show: Bristol, Canterbury (Heritage Centre, Poor Priest Hospital), Carlisle, Exeter, Hereford, King's Lynn, Lincoln, Newcastle-upon-Tyne, Oxford, Southampton (God's House Tower), Winchester, York (Yorkshire Museum).

Remains of deserted villages

Gainsthorpe, near Hibaldstow, Lincolnshire

Godwick, near Tittleshall, Norfolk

Hound Tor, near Widecombe in the Moor, Devon

Nether Adber, near Marston Magna, Somerset

Wharram Percy, near Wharram le Street, Yorkshire

Reconstructed houses

Cosmeston, near Penarth, Glamorgan

Weald & Downland Open Air Museum, near Chichester, West Sussex

Manor houses

Ightham Mote, Ightham, Kent

Scotney Castle, near Lamberhurst, Kent

Stokesay Castle, Shropshire

West Bromwich Old Hall, West Midlands

Young Archaeologists Club

If you are interested in finding out more about archaeology, you might like to join the Young Archaeologists Club, United House, Piccadilly, York YO1 1PQ.

Glossary

Adze A carpenter's tool for trimming the surface of timber.

Analysis Finding out what something is made of; often in a laboratory.

Cauldron A large cooking pot.

Cesspit A pit below a lavatory.

Chivalry The rules saying how a knight should fight bravely and fairly, and how he should behave towards women.

Fuller's earth Clay-like earth that absorbs grease from wool.

Glaze A glassy coating that makes pots and tiles shiny.

Hospice A medieval hospital.

Inventory A list of possessions or equipment.

Kiln A large oven for baking pottery or tiles.

Lathe A machine for shaping wood by turning.

Malnutrition Not getting enough of the right food to keep well.

Parchment A sheepskin prepared for writing on.

Pollute To make something dirty.

Potter's wheel A special wheel on which a pot spins when being shaped.

Rickets A children's disease caused by lack of Vitamin D. The bones become soft.

Riveted Joined by metal pins.

Scurvy A disease with bleeding of the gums due to a lack of Vitamin C.

Tag A little bit of metal rolled round the end of a lace.

Tournament A fight between knights on horseback in front of a large crowd of people.

Wattle and daub A wall made out of woven branches covered with mud mixed with chopped straw or dung.

Books to read

Bagley, J. *Medieval People* (Batsford, 1986)

Ross, S. *Chaucer and the Middle Ages* (Wayland, 1985)

Ross, S. *A Medieval Serf* (Wayland, 1986)

Ross, S. *A Medieval Monk* (Wayland, 1986)

Unstead, R. J. *The Middle Ages* (Black, 1979)

The following books are part of a series on archaeology published by Shire:

Allen Brown, R. *Castles* (1985)

Hall, D. *Medieval Fields* (1987)

Haslam, J. *Medieval Pottery in Britain* (1984), *Early Medieval Towns in Britain* (1985)

Hindle, B. *Medieval Roads* (1982)

Hinton, D. *Medieval Jewellery* (1982)

Rowley, T. and Wood, J. *Deserted Villages* (1982)

Wilson, D. *Moated Sites* (1985)

Index